Pregnancy—

PITFALLS, PRINCIPLES, AND PEARLS

TOBE MOMAH MD

Diplomat American Board of Family Medicine

Foreword by MacMillan W. Rodney, MD

WestBow
PRESS
A DIVISION OF THOMAS NELSON

WestBow Press books may be ordered through booksellers or by contacting:

WestBow Press
A Division of Thomas Nelson
1663 Liberty Drive
Bloomington, IN 47403
www.westbowpress.com
1-(866) 928-1240

The information, ideas, and suggestions in this book are not intended as a substitute for professional medical advice. Before following any suggestions contained in this book, you should consult your personal physician. Neither the author nor the publisher shall be liable or responsible for any loss or damage allegedly arising as a consequence of your use or application of any information or suggestions in this book.

ISBN: 978-1-4497-6210-0 (sc)
ISBN: 978-1-4497-6211-7 (e)

Library of Congress Control Number: 2012914371

Printed in the United States of America

WestBow Press rev. date: 08/23/2012

Pregnancy-

PITFALLS, PRINCIPLES, AND PEARLS

TOBE MOMAH MD
Diplomat American Board of Family Medicine

Foreword by MacMillan W. Rodney, MD

WESTBOW
P R E S S
A DIVISION OF THOMAS NELSON

WestBow Press books may be ordered through booksellers or by contacting:

WestBow Press
A Division of Thomas Nelson
1663 Liberty Drive
Bloomington, IN 47403
www.westbowpress.com
1-(866) 928-1240

The information, ideas, and suggestions in this book are not intended as a substitute for professional medical advice. Before following any suggestions contained in this book, you should consult your personal physician. Neither the author nor the publisher shall be liable or responsible for any loss or damage allegedly arising as a consequence of your use or application of any information or suggestions in this book.

ISBN: 978-1-4497-6210-0 (sc)
ISBN: 978-1-4497-6211-7 (e)

Library of Congress Control Number: 2012914371

Printed in the United States of America

WestBow Press rev. date: 08/23/2012

CONTENTS

Preface   *vii*

Foreword   *ix*

Acknowledgments   *xi*

Chapter 1: The Newly Pregnant Patient   1

Chapter 2: Preconception Care   5

Chapter 3: The First Month   12

Chapter 4: Causes of Miscarriage   17

Chapter 5: Where Not to Go in Pregnancy!   23

Chapter 6: When the Treatment Is Worse Than the Disease!   27

Chapter 7: 100 Simple Steps to a Successful Pregnancy   31

Chapter 8: Blunders in Birthing!   41

Chapter 9: Starting a House   49

Chapter 10: When All Else Fails   53

PREFACE

Maternal mortality has barely improved in the last thirty years. This is in spite of cutting-edge technology and trillions of dollars invested. The global maternal mortality ratio (that is the number of maternal deaths per one hundred thousand live births) declined by only 2.3 percent between 1990 and 2008, and over one thousand pregnant or recently post-partum women die daily from pregnancy-related complications. Most of these deaths could have been prevented if the simple concepts discussed in this book were applied.

From my medical tutelage in Nigeria, to my mission trips in Ethiopia, and now in modern America practicing full-spectrum family medicine, I have seen a needless waste of pregnant women's lives from inadvertent and preventable causes—but it doesn't have to be this way. If the three hundred fifty-eight thousand women, who died following pregnancy or childbirth in 2008, had access to the information in this book many would still be alive today!

This book covers the entire nine-month pregnancy and teaches mothers-to-be how to apply simple, down-to-earth principles, laced with medical pearls, and avoid the common pitfalls many make in pregnancy.

FOREWORD

I am one of the oldest family medicine doctors still delivering babies and taking night calls. I was an academically tenured professor for over twenty years, but I started a bilingual private practice in 1999. Our focus is family care including obstetrics. The need and opportunity for obstetrical family medicine is so great that, even in an over-doctored American urban area, our coalition of family physicians in private practice has grown to over two thousand deliveries per year. But it took the political support of the Dean and Chair to achieve our hospital privileges. If you can unlock these, there is a bright future for obstetrical family medicine and the material included in this book by Dr. Momah.

Generic primary care skills are not sufficient for the acute care needs of underserved communities. Most vulnerable is the pregnant woman and her delivery. Despite the heritage of family medicine, many academic family medicine programs have only a token commitment from their faculty. This shortchanges the professional abilities of young physicians who would otherwise aspire to provide delivery and newborn care. Thank you Dr. Momah for this wonderful book.

Wm. MacMillan Rodney, MD
Private Practice Professor and Chair
Surgical Family Medicine Obstetrics
Medicos Memphis, Nashville, and International

ACKNOWLEDGMENTS

I would like to thank Mrs. Burke, an astounding eighty-four-year-old retired teacher, who went above and beyond the call of duty to help edit this book. Without her, there would still be multiple errors in the manuscript—and maybe no book published at all.

My wife of nine years, and the love of my life, endured long nights and endless weekends without me while I wrote this book. She gave her full cooperation and even called my non-committal stand to correction when I failed to achieve deadlines or aspire to perfection in my writing. To her love, passion, and endless search for adventure and challenges, I remain grateful. She was a sounding board for a lot of material used in this book.

My pastor, Shane Warren, captured this book's essence in his sermons and gave me a future filled with expectancy. He showed me the power of relationships and stirred our church to see ourselves as high-net-worth caliber assets and not just church folk!

My family including Dad and Mom, Dr. Sam and Mrs. Momah; and brothers and sisters including Emeka, Nkem, Ada, Amaka and their respective spouses and children stood shoulder-to-shoulder with me while writing this book. They never failed to give support anytime I needed it (which was often), and for that, I am eternally grateful.

Finally, I would like to acknowledge my publishers WestBow Press for their awe-inspiring work and dedication to this book. My prayer is that God would bless all those involved in this project, and as they made it happen for me, God will make it happen in their lives too, in Jesus' name.

Tobe Momah, MD

If God sets you up, you become unstoppable!

CHAPTER 1

The Newly Pregnant Patient

Children are an heritage of the Lord and the fruit of
the womb is his reward. As arrows are in the hand of a
mighty man so are children of the youth.
—Psalm 127:3-4

Pregnancy is the most common medical condition a female will ever encounter, with 92 percent of women between fifteen and forty-four years of age carrying at least one episode of pregnancy to term.[1] At least 120 million women will carry their pregnancies to term this year world-wide, and of that number, only 5 percent (among teenagers) and 50 percent (among adults) are planned!

Human understanding of how the fetus is formed is still shrouded in mystery. Jeremiah 1:5 says, "Before [God] formed thee in the belly He knew thee," and Isaiah 44:2 says, "The Lord made thee and formed thee from the womb." Job 10:8 adds that God's "hands have made us and fashioned us together round about . . . [and He has] clothed us with skin and flesh and fenced us with bones and sinews." One thing that's certain, however, is that you and I are "fearfully and wonderfully made [and] marvelous are His works" (Psalm 139:14).

It takes six days for a fertilized egg (called a zygote) to implant in the uterus, but it will take at least twenty to twenty-eight days after her last menstrual period for a woman to know she is pregnant.

Preconception Interventions

Even before a woman knows she is pregnant, medical science recommends proven ways to increase health, such as taking folic and prenatal vitamins, avoiding cigarettes and alcohol, and getting vaccinated against rubella, tetanus, diphtheria, and influenza.

Regular exercise is highly encouraged in the preconception period. A physically fit woman is a more fertile woman! Women with a body mass index (BMI) above thirty have a threefold increased risk of preterm deliveries, serious pregnancy complications, and finally, death.

A woman preparing for pregnancy must avoid narcotics or other forms of drugs, including cocaine, heroin, marijuana, amphetamines, or prescription drug abuse. She must also (obviously) stop using any and all forms of contraception and time her sexual experience with her ovulation periods.

Signs and Symptoms of Pregnancy

Most newly pregnant women will seek medical attention because of a missed menstrual period. In addition to laboratory testing, physical signs and symptoms are useful ways of confirming a pregnancy.

The symptoms include fatigue, nausea, and breast tenderness, while the signs include amenorrhea; skin changes, including chloasma (darkening of the face) and linea nigra (hyperpigmentation of the abdominal midline); and softening of the uterine and cervical tissue (Hegar's sign).

Other less specific signs and symptoms include an aversion to certain types of food, like fried foods and coffee; increased frequency of urination; constipation; mood disorders; and implantation bleeding (spotting from the vagina about ten days after fertilization).

Misdiagnosing a Pregnancy

A twenty-eight-year-old patient of mine was already a single parent (of a five-year-old girl) when she walked into my office asking for authorization from me to enable her dermatologist to give her medicine for acne.

The urine pregnancy test was read as negative by my staff, and I wrote a letter stating she was not pregnant and, considering she was using two contraceptive techniques, was suitable for Accutane. She saw her dermatologist a week later, and thankfully, he did another pregnancy test, which returned a positive result. He refused to give her the Accutane pills.

Needless to say, the patient was very upset. However, during our conversation, she confessed to having recent unprotected intercourse.

I learned an invaluable lesson: the readings of urine pregnancy tests are operator-dependent and are not 100 percent accurate. If you read the urine pregnancy test kit earlier than the mandatory timeframe indicated, you may obtain a false negative result.

Poor Preparation Makes for Poor Performance.

CHAPTER 2

Preconception Care

> Which of you, intending to build a tower, sits not down
> first and counts the cost whether he have sufficient to
> finish it? Lest haply, after he hath laid the foundation,
> and is not able to finish it, all that behold it begin to
> mock him.
> —Luke 14:28-29

There are some basic things you must do before pregnancy if you want to deliver a healthy child. These include the following:

1. Stop Taking Over-the-Counter Medications

Stop taking any over-the-counter (OTC) medications, and postpone any elective procedures until you consult your obstetrician. Medications are classified into categories A, B, C, D, and X based on their propensity to cause teratogenicity. Category X drugs are not fit for use in pregnancy, and category A drugs are suitable and safe in pregnancy. Drugs in categories B, C, and D have a progressively worse level of damaging the fetus. Examples of these category of medications and their designated complications in human and animal species are shown in Table 1 below.

It was only until thalidomide use (the drug used for morning sickness and anxiety in the early 1960s) resulted in severe cases of deformed babies that an awareness of the side effects of these medications was initiated. Thalidomide caused limb reduction defects in one-third of infants exposed to it and prompted the initiation of drug regulation in pregnancy.

Even today, as many as 86 percent of pregnant women use non-obstetrician-prescribed medications, with 30 percent of them using more than four non-recommended prescriptions. Six of the top ten drugs used by this category of patients were OTC medications.

The most commonly used drugs that cause fetal damage include alcohol, androgens, angiotensin-converting enzyme (ACE) inhibitors, angiotensin II receptor blockers (ARB), anticonvulsants (including trimethadione, valproic acid, phenytoin, and carbabmazepine), chemotherapeutic agents, iodides, isotrietinoin, lithium, tetracycline, and warfarin. Thankfully, thalidomide and diethylstilbesterol are now banned.

Table 1

US FDA Pharmaceutical Pregnancy Categories	
Pregnancy Category A	Adequate and well-controlled human studies have failed to demonstrate a risk to the fetus in the first trimester of pregnancy (and there is no evidence of risk in later trimesters).
Pregnancy Category B	Animal reproduction studies have failed to demonstrate a risk to the fetus, and there are no adequate and well-controlled studies in pregnant women, or animal studies have shown an adverse effect, but adequate and well-controlled studies in pregnant women have failed to demonstrate a risk to the fetus in any trimester.
Pregnancy Category C	Animal reproduction studies have shown an adverse effect on the fetus, and there are no adequate and well-controlled studies in humans, but potential benefits may warrant use of the drug in pregnant women despite potential risks.

Pregnancy Category D	There is positive evidence of human fetal risk based on adverse reaction data from investigational or marketing experience or studies in humans, but potential benefits may warrant use of the drug in pregnant women despite potential risks.
Pregnancy Category X	Studies in animals or humans have demonstrated fetal abnormalities and/or there is positive evidence of human fetal risk based on adverse reaction data from investigational or marketing experience, and the risks involved in use of the drug in pregnant women clearly outweigh potential benefits.

2. Use Folic Acid Daily

Start taking at least 4 mg of folic acid daily, as it is proven to reduce the incidence of neural tube defects by 50-70 percent. It is protective when taken in preconception, as the neural tube develops as early as the third week of pregnancy. About three thousand women develop complications of neural tube defects annually, but this can be easily prevented by supplementing their diet (even before conception) with folate-rich foods, such as vegetables and fruits.

In the United States, only 40 percent of pregnant women reported routine use of folic acid, and those less likely to use it were nonwhite, young, and less educated.[2] Just by taking 4 mg of folic acid daily, a pregnant woman with a past history of neural tube defect in earlier pregnancies, can reduce a future episode by 72 percent.

Other patients who should take the 4 mg daily dose of folic acid include pregnant women with multiple gestations (more than one fetus), those taking anticonvulsant medications, and anyone who used oral contraceptive pills (OCPs) before conception.

3. Avoid Substance Abuse

While contemplating pregnancy, preterm precautions should include avoidance of toxic substances like cigarettes, alcohol, and substances of abuse, including amphetamines, opiates, cocaine, and marijuana. Because greater than 50 percent of pregnancies in the Western world are unplanned, many women unknowingly expose their fetuses to toxic substances in their first six to eight weeks of life.

To date, 20-25 percent of American women use cigarettes, 8 percent abuse substances, and 7 percent or more abuse alcohol (more than two glasses of alcohol daily). The level of alcohol intake responsible for fetal alcohol syndrome (which can include central nervous dysfunction, growth deficiencies, facial abnormalities, and mental retardation) is anything above one drink of alcohol per day. Abstinence from alcohol is strictly recommended for all pregnant women.

Cigarette smoking during pregnancy causes low birth weight (LBW), sudden infant death syndrome (SIDS), abruptio placenta, newborn asthma, middle ear infections, and preterm deliveries. These issues are caused by cigarette consumption either actively or passively (if exposed to nicotine fumes for greater than two hours).

According to the Substance Abuse and Mental health Services administration 2003 survey, 4.3 percent of pregnant women between the ages of fifteen and forty-four years reported using illicit drugs a month before the survey.[3] This was especially common in the fifteen to twenty-five years age bracket (with a prevalence rate of 8 percent) with Marijuana the most commonly used illicit substance at 76 percent of the total. Common complications from use of illicit drugs in pregnancy include spontaneous abortion, Low Birth Weight births, preterm deliveries, abruption placenta and central nervous system (CNS) defects such as cerebral infarcts and microcephaly.

4. Get Vaccinated

Live vaccinations such as varicella (chicken pox), bacilli Calmette-Guérin (BCG), smallpox, yellow fever, measles, rubella, and mumps must be done at least three months before conception to avoid transferring live strains of the virus to the fetus. Killed vaccines like influenza, tetanus, pertussis, and diphtheria are safe during pregnancy as they pose no maternal or fetal risks. Vaccines like hepatitis B can also be safely administered during pregnancy, if required.

The only times vaccinations during pregnancy aren't recommended are vaccination with the smallpox virus or the mumps, measles, rubella and varicella (MMRV) vaccines. The vaccination with smallpox on the fetus is very harmful and should not even be administered to a household contact of a pregnant woman. Only the killed influenza virus vaccine should be administered in pregnant women and is limited to women who will be pregnant in influenza season (between October and March every year).

New guidelines from the American Committee on immunization practice (ACIP) recommend giving the diptheria, tetanus, and acellular pertussis (TdaP) vaccine to adolescents who are pregnant and have not previously received the vaccine. It should preferably be administered during the third or late second trimester (after twenty weeks gestation). It reduces infantile pertussis rates as they receive maternal antibodies to pertussis during the fetal period.[4]

5. Avoid Physical/Occupational Abuse

Occupational adjustments include avoiding stressful work conditions such as working more than ten hours daily or one hundred hours or more a week, prolonged standing of more than six hours per shift, heavy lifting, and excessive noise. Women who work too many hours or are impacted by these factors have increased episodes of preterm labor.

Women who are pregnant should also be advised to avoid contact sports, deep sea diving, and other at-risk competitive sports. They can, however, continue aerobics, swimming, walking, bicycling, dancing, and non-competitive tennis.

Notes:

1. CDC, "Fertility, Family Planning, and Women's Health: New Data From the 1995 National Survey of Family Growth," (1997). Washington, DC: National Center for Health Statistics.

2. CDC, "Use of Vitamins Containing Folic Acid among Women of Child Bearing Age—United States," 2004, *MMWR Morb Mortal Wkly Rep* 53:847-850, 2004.

3. CDC. "Recommendations for Using Smallpox Vaccine in a Pre-event Vaccination Program: Supplemental Recommendations of the Advisory Committee on Immunization Practices (ACIP) and the Healthcare Infection Control Practices Advisory Committee (HICPAC)," *MMWR* 2003; 52 (No. RR-7).

4. "Vaccines for Children: ACIP-VFC Vaccine Resolutions: Vaccines to Prevent Pertussis, Tetanus and Diphtheria," Resolution No. 6/11-2, http://www.cdc.gov/vaccines/programs/vfc/downloads/resolutions/0611dtap.pdf.

God is a finisher.
He never abandons what He begins!

CHAPTER 3

The First Month

When I begin I will also make an end.
—1 Samuel 3:12

The last menstrual period (LMP) determines the age of the fetus chronologically; it also gives an estimate of the expected day of delivery by adding 280 days to the LMP. Urine tests can diagnose pregnancy 98 percent of the time if taken one week after implantation of the zygote (which is, on average, about four weeks after the LMP).

In addition to extensive lab work, one thing routinely done in the first month is the Papanicolau (PAP) smear of the cervix (if not done in the last twelve months). Pregnant patients must also have an all encompassing history and physical exam highlighting prior pregnancies, early terminations, family history, genetic history, social history, and list any medical or surgical condition the patient suffers from or has suffered from.

It is also important in the first trimester to refer patients for dietary and nutritional counseling, dental examinations, and to a social worker. This enables the health system to identify any social or physical issues that need to be addressed, and if necessary, ensure early intervention.

Referrals in the First Month

1. Nutritionist

The normal range of weight gain in pregnancy varies for each woman (see Table 2). Nutritionists generally advise that women should consume only the required calories (which is 150 extra calories per day in the first trimester and 300-500 extra calories per day in the last two trimesters) and highlight the need for a balanced diet for proper fetal development.

Nutritionists also highlight certain things a patient should avoid and these include more than twelve ounces of tuna per week (as excess mercury from King Mackerel, tilefish, monkfish, swordfish, and shark leads to neurological damage in the fetus). Other things to avoid include greater than 300 mg per day of caffeine (as it leads to preterm labor, spontaneous abortion, and slows growth) and non-pasteurized milk, cheese, or poorly cooked meat products (as that could lead to infections).

Pregnant women should also be educated on an unusual craving for non-nutritive substances such as clay, starch, ice, or dirt. This craving is called Pica and occurs commonly in pregnancy and causes iron deficiency anemia by binding the iron and so preventing its absorption. Another problem in pregnancy is an unusual food craving called citta where the pregnant woman indulges in large amounts of non-nutritive foods.

Vegetarians are prone to developing iron, protein, calcium, iodine, zinc, and vitamin B12 deficiencies during pregnancy and may require supplements. There may be a need to avoid fried foods in the first trimester especially in those with *Hyperemesis Gravidarum*, a condition characterized by incessant nausea and vomiting. Instead patients can eat dry carbohydrates (like bread), low-fat foods, and avoid use of heavy smelling seasonings.

Patients should also be counseled to avoid handling cat feces, soil, or undercooked meat (such as lamb, pork, venison or beef), because these could endanger the life of the fetus, especially during the third trimester of pregnancy.

Table 2

How Much Weight Should You Gain During Pregnancy?		
Prepregnancy Weight Status	*Body Mass Index (BMI)**	*Weight Gain (pounds)*
Underweight	Less than 18.5	28-40
Normal weight	18.5-24.9	25-35
Overweight	25.0-29.9	15-25
Obese	30 or more	11-20
*You can find out your BMI by going to https://www. yourpregnancyandchildbirth.com/topics.php?page=nutrition		
Data from Institute of Medicine (United States). Weight gain during pregnancy: reexamining the guidelines. Washington, DC: National Academies Press; 2009.		

2. Social Worker

Patient safety and healthy surroundings cannot be over-emphasized in the well being of the fetus. A social worker will ensure that the baby will have a safe and welcoming home when born, and if necessary, assist the mother, by providing financial aid and counseling to achieve that.

The social worker is also instrumental in inquiring about any verbal and physical abuse during pregnancy and can provide a safe haven, through government or community support, for the pregnant patient and her baby.

3. Dentist

A higher number of pre-term, low-birth-weight babies occur in patients with periodontal disease. A referral to the dentist is intended to educate patients on dental hygiene, and if necessary, dental work under local anesthesia can be done.

Perinatal gingivitis is relatively common, occurring in up to half of pregnant women, and can cause up to seven times higher incidence of preterm deliveries. Expectant mothers are, therefore, encouraged to have existing tooth decay treated during their pregnancy as long as it does not entail general anesthesia. Routine oral hygiene measures such as flossing, use of fluoride toothpaste, and daily brushing should be continued.

4. Sonographer

A first trimester sonogram is routinely requested even though no benefit to fetal outcome has been demonstrated. The main benefit, however, of early sonograms is the provision of a more accurate estimate of gestational age, diagnosis of multiple gestation pregnancies, and the earlier detection of otherwise unsuspected fetal anomalies.

A sonogram done in the first trimester confirms a fetal gestational age to be within four days, while one done in the second trimester gives a window period of within twelve days. It is least accurate when measured in the third trimester with a gestational age of within twenty-one days.

Sonograms are also useful in determining cervical length, assessing fetal wellbeing (using amniotic fluid quantity), and ensuring early intervention as required. Sonograms are safe in pregnancy and develop their images from sound energy that is converted to heat distributed in body tissues.

When there is loss, God restores.
And where there is gain, God replenishes.

CHAPTER 4

Causes of Miscarriage

Ye shall serve the Lord your God and He shall bless thy
bread and thy water and take sickness away from the
midst of thee. There shall nothing cast their young, nor
be barren, in the land (and) the number of thy days He
will fulfill.
—Exodus 23:25

The first trimester is considered the "holy grail" of pregnancy.
The seven systems of the body form during this time, so even the
mildest infringements like harmful medications or toxins can be
lethal to fetal life at that stage.

Days fifteen to fifty-six of gestation are the most critical period
for organogenesis in the newborn. The heart starts beating at twenty
days of fetal life and the neural tube completes development at twenty-
one days of intrapartum fetal life.

At this stage most pregnant women are not even aware they
are pregnant and therefore many insult themselves (and their fetus)
unknowingly. There are several medical terms for miscarriage, such
as missed, complete or incomplete abortion, and it occurs in about
20 percent of pregnancies.

Common Causes of Miscarriage

1. Infection

Maternal infections (especially in the first trimester) should be avoided at this critical point of fetal life. Infections such as Lupus may lead to congenital heart block while the "ToRCH" group of infections (that is toxoplasmosis, rubella, cytomegalovirus and herpes genitalis) can cause cataracts, deafness, and mental challenges.

Other infections that may be transmitted to the fetus from the mother include sexually transmitted infections such as human immunodeficiency virus (HIV), syphilis, human papilloma virus (HPV), genital herpes simplex virus (HSV), trichomoniasis, chlamydia, and gonorrhea.

The most common maternal infection in the first trimester of pregnancy is asymptomatic bacteriuria (ASB), which occurs in 2-10 percent of all pregnancies. It should be checked for at every prenatal visit and, if found, treatment should be started with safe antibiotics.

The most lethal of all infections in pregnancy is a vertically transmitted maternal infection seen in 30% of pregnant women called Group B Streptococcus (GBS) neonatal infection. It causes 10% mortality in early onset GBS infections, preterm labor, possible miscarriage and is responsible for 15% of all ASB's in pregnancy. It should be screened for at 35- 37 weeks and if positive treated intrapartum with appropriate antibiotics.

2. Toxins

Any toxin, whether environmental (like lead, mercury, or organic solvents), substances of abuse (such as smoking, drinking, or illicit drugs), or herbs like St. John's Wort or Kava can leave the fetus with permanent disabilities.

Women exposed to high levels of lead may develop fetuses with central nerve system damage, hydrocephalus, skin tags, hemangiomas, or lymphangiomas. Lead can also cause miscarriages or stillbirth.

Mercury toxicity, derived from inhaling elemental mercury in mercury thermometers, fluorescent light bulbs, dental amalgam fillings, electrical equipment, or elemental mercury, is associated with stillbirths, birth defects, and spontaneous abortions in pregnant women.

3. Unauthorized Medications

Any medicinal product taken during pregnancy must be first approved by your obstetrician or family physician. In the first trimester, the most commonly prescribed medications include acetaminophen, folic acid, and prenatal vitamins. Non-steroidal anti-inflammatory drugs (NSAIDS) are not recommended due to medical complications in fetal life including perinatal mortality, neonatal hemorrhage, decreased birth weight, prolonged gestation and labor, and possible birth defects[3].

Another common blunder in the first trimester of pregnancy is the use of vitamin A or multivitamins containing vitamin A. It is the only vitamin curtailed for use in pregnant patients because at doses greater than 8,000 IU/day, it is associated with craniofacial, central nervous system, and cardiac defects.

Other unauthorized medications include tetracyclines—a macrolide—which chelates on fetal dentition as early as the fifth month of pregnancy and causes yellowing of dentition. Quinolones, which impair cartilage development in children, should also be avoided in pregnancy.

Commonly used medications that are safe in pregnancy include Budesonide inhaled or nasal spray for asthma, Nitrofurantoin or Penicillin, ampicillin, cephalosporins, Augmentin for bladder or respiratory infections, Dextromethrophan for cough, Metamucil, Docusate, Milk of magnesia, Polyethyelene glycol for constipation, Insulin, Glyburide, Metformin for Diabetes, Loperamide, Simethicone for diarrhea, Ranitidine, Cimetidine for Gastroesophageal reflux disease (GERD), Chlorpheniramine, Diphenhydramine, Acetaminophen for Hay fever, sneezing, runny nose, itchy watery eyes, Anusol suppositories for hemorrhoids, Methyldopa for High blood pressure, Bromocriptine and Carbergoline for Hyperprolactinemia, Levothyroxine for Hypothyroidism, Acyclovir for Herpes, Azthitromycin, Cepaholosporins,Clindamycin, Erythromycin, Penicillins, Metronidazole for infections and <u>Doxylamine</u> for insomnia.

4. Urinary or Vaginal Tract Commensals

These are not sexually transmitted infections but rather microorganisms that become overwhelming in an immuno-compromised state, such as pregnancy, and include asymptomatic group B beta streptococci and vaginal candidiasis.

Some women develop a shift of vaginal flora (secondary to douching or poor hygiene) toward alkalosis and develop bacterial vaginosis (secondary to *Gadnarella vaginalis*) in their vaginal tract. Bacterial vaginosis is the most common vaginal infection (affecting as many as 15-20 percent of the general female population) and leads to increased preterm labor, spontaneous abortions, chorioamnionitis, and post-cesarean-section endometritis. It can be treated with metronidazole or tinidazole with recurrent and resistant varieties treated with Clindamycin.[1]

Vulvovaginal candidiasis is very common in pregnancy and affects as many as fourteen million women annually (in the United States). It is caused by a fungal species including *Candida albicans*, *Candida tropicalis*, and *Candida Glabrata*. Though it is annoying, it has no long-term fetal effects. It should be treated by only topical "azoles" as oral therapy can harm the fetus.

Group B streptococcus (GBS) occurs in at least 30 percent of pregnant women and when found during the first trimester, requires immediate antibiotic treatment. This prevents neonatal GBS infections, which can be fatal. If untreated, it can lead to higher risks for preterm labor, spontaneous abortions, and other complications.

5. High Coffee Intake

Coffee is drunk by about 70 percent of western women, and unfortunately, many of them drink during pregnancy. Anything greater than three cups a day of coffee (or 300 mg/day) will increase miscarriage rates by as much as 100 percent in the first trimester.[2] A reduction to at most one cup of caffeine a day is advocated in pregnancy. Other products that contain caffeine (such as sodas and teas) should also be used sparingly.

Notes:

1. Center for disease control and prevention, "Sexually Transmitted Diseases Treatment Guidelines," 2006, *MMWR* 55:51-52, 2006.
2. Infante-Rivard C., Fernandez A, Gutheir R., et al., "Fetal Loss Associated with Caffeine Intake before and during Pregnancy," *JAMA* 270:2940-2943, 1993.
3. Collins E. Maternal and fetal effects of acetaminophen and salicylates in pregnancy. *Obstet Gynecol.* 1981;585 Suppl:57S–62S.

Who you join determines what you enjoy!

CHAPTER 5

Where Not to Go in Pregnancy!

If men who are fighting hit a pregnant woman and she
gives birth prematurely but there is no serious injury,
the offender must be fined whatever the woman's
husband demands and the court allows.
—Exodus 21:22

There are very few places a pregnant woman can't go during pregnancy. Having said that, however, there are still areas where unnecessary demise of the fetus can occur and we are counseled, in the Word of God, to be wise.

In Exodus 21:22, for example, we see that unnecessary exposure to conflict can prevent the healthy delivery of a baby. Exposing unborn babies to conflict can drastically affect their future. Just like John the Baptist received the Spirit in the womb of his mother, by the adulation of Mary (see Luke 1:41), an unborn fetus can be affected positively or negatively right there in the womb.

Theatres of Conflict

1) Whirlpools and Swimming Pools

Pregnant women should avoid using whirlpools, saunas, and hot tubs above 101°F as an elevated body temperature can increase the risk of birth defects. Swimming is permitted as long as adequate measures to avoid transmission of microorganisms into the vagina are taken. In patients with recurrent miscarriages or repeat pre-term labor incidents, a shower or gentle bath in a tub is recommended with no douching or vaginal insertion.

2) Gyms and Strenuous Sports

Strenuous exercise in pregnancy should be limited to aerobics or casual walking, jogging, or tennis playing. Contact sports, high-altitude sports, and competitive sports that involve collision such as boxing, field hockey, rugby, ice hockey, martial arts, rodeo, soccer, and wrestling should be avoided. Exercises that involve being on your back and using the Valsalva maneuver (holding the nose, closing the mouth, and blowing air to try and pop your ears) should also be avoided.

Sports such as parachute jumping, hang gliding, rock climbing, springboard diving, fencing, power weight lifting, or long-distance running should also be avoided.

3) Radiation Exposure

Every pregnant woman, except those in critical need, should avoid exposure to radioactive sources like mammograms, x-rays, computerized tomography (CT) scans, and fluoroscopy during pregnancy. If radiation is necessary, make sure to inform the caregiver and they will shield the chest/abdomen to avoid radiation waves.

Magnetic Resonance Imaging (MRIs) and sonograms are, on the other hand, not radioactive emitters and safe in pregnant women. MRIs with gadolinium contrast could, however, lead to nephrogenic sclerosing fibrosis and should be avoided (except in an emergency) during pregnancy.

4) Airplanes and High-Altitude Flights

Airlines are universally disallowed from bringing pregnant women on board after thirty-six weeks of pregnancy. There are a few exceptions to this rule (as stipulated by the International Civil Aviation Organization), but even these must be accompanied by a doctor's letter explaining the necessity for travel.

The reason for restricting air travel in pregnant women is their increased risk of pre-term labor and worsening fetal hypoxia at those advanced weeks of gestation. These restrictions are not applicable to ground transport vehicles like buses, coaches, trains, or ships.

5) Toxic Exposures

Certain toxic substances can harm the fetus and pregnant patients should avoid them. Solvents such as Toluene, xylene, thinners, and paint strippers, which are widely used in the paint industry, or chemotherapeutic agents may increase the rate of miscarriage and birth defects and should be avoided. Even heavy metals such as iron, mercury, and cadmium adversely affect fetal neurological development and should be avoided.

6) Over-Tasking Work Environments

Employment does not increase the risk of pre-term delivery or mortality, but excessive work can adversely affect the outcome of pregnancy. These include working more than one hundred hours a week, prolonged standing (greater than six hours per shift), heavy lifting, excessive noise, or mental stress.

The road to hell is sometimes paved with good intentions!

CHAPTER 6

When the Treatment Is Worse Than the Disease!

Be not righteous over much; neither make thyself over wise: why shouldest thou destroy thyself?
—Ecclesiastes 7:16

Many cultures are replete with diverse traditions during pregnancy. The Indians believe, for example that eating eggs, papaya, and pineapples can cause an abortion, while the Aztec Mexicans believe that a pregnant woman should not view the eclipse or step out in the sun during an eclipse because an eclipse represents a bite on the face of the moon and would cause a cleft palate on the baby's face.

A widespread belief that is wrong and erroneous is that lifting your hands above your head while pregnant will strangle the fetus with the umbilical cord. Other mythologies say a woman should not stand in a doorway while pregnant or she will have trouble having the baby.

While many of these beliefs are unfounded myths that are folksy and rooted in traditions, a few medical therapies that are worse than the symptoms they are supposed to cure have also, in error, been implemented with calamitous consequences.

The Thalidomide Tragedy

The thalidomide tragedy started with the birth of a deformed baby on December 25, 1956. It went on to affect almost twenty thousand children across Europe, Asia, Canada, Australia, and Latin America with congenital abnormalities at birth including the absence or shortening of limbs, deafness, absence of the muscles of the eyes and face, and malformation of internal organs including the heart, bowels, uterus, and gallbladder.

Thalidomide was synthesized in 1956 and marketed in 1957 as a "wonder drug" capable of treating morning sickness, as commonly seen in the first trimester of pregnancy. The treatment was however worse than the disease as more than ten thousand babies in forty-six countries were born with multiple deformities and more than half died in the process!

After multiple litigations across the world, an out of court settlement was reached with the makers, Grunenthal pharmaceuticals of Germany. The US Congress then enacted laws requiring tests for safety during pregnancy before a drug can receive approval for sale in the United States, and this was followed suit by other western countries.

Thalidomide is currently a restricted prescription that is only used in very select cases.

The Diethylstilbestrol (DES) Dilemma

In 1971, a new drug formulated in the 1930s by British scientists, was found to have caused seven cases of clear cell carcinoma of the vagina. The initial uses of DES were for atrophic vaginitis, menopausal symptoms, and postpartum lactation initially.

In 1947, it was approved as an estrogen replacement therapy for menopausal women and also to prevent adverse pregnancy outcomes in women with a history of miscarriage.

Its treatment was actually worse than the miscarriage it tried to avoid. It has caused millions of women worldwide to undergo disfiguring vaginal reconstruction and hysterectomies due to a diagnosis of clear cell carcinoma of the vagina. If the mother of a child took DES during her pregnancy, it delayed manifestation in the child for another twenty years.

The majority of DES complications included infertility, spontaneous abortion, preterm delivery, loss of second-trimester pregnancy, ectopic pregnancy, preeclampsia, stillbirth, early menopause, and grade 2 or higher cervical intraepithelial neoplasia. The worst outcome, however, is in clear cell carcinoma of the vagina because of its insidious growth and poor response to chemo or radiation therapy.

Twin Troubles!

Mary Slessor was a Scottish missionary who spent forty years working in the hinterland of the Efik in the nation of Nigeria. She was grieved by the murder of twins in Calabar and set about rescuing them. She traversed the Efik and Ibo nations, canvassing for this cruel culture to be dropped.

The culture of killing twins thrived because the tribes thought that twins were a result of a curse caused by an evil spirit who fathered one of the children. It (twinning) was a "disease" to their primitive mentality but the treatment—brutally murdering both twins—was worse!

Eventually, Mary Slessor rescued hundreds of babies and established schools and vocational institutes for these abandoned children and their shamed mothers to venture into and learn a trade or profession.

The outcome of this was the establishment of Christianity as the predominant religion of the area and the enthronement of Mary Slessor as a judge over the people and the Queen's representative to south-south Nigeria.

She never got married but on her death in 1915, after forty years in the harsh hinterland of Calabar region, she was surrounded by many adopted children whom she had single-handily saved.

Success is not the absence of danger but the presence of God.

CHAPTER 7

100 Simple Steps to a Successful Pregnancy

She shall be saved in childbearing if she continue in
faith and charity and holiness with sobriety.
—1 Timothy 2:15

1. Eat a balanced diet consisting of all five major nutrient groups including carbohydrates, protein, fats and oil, vitamins, and minerals.
2. Avoid any exposure to cigarette smoke—first-hand or second-hand.
3. Avoid any substances of abuse including heroine, cocaine, marijuana, LSD, amphetamine, or nicotine.
4. Do not insert any inanimate objects into your vagina.
5. Maintain light exercises (like walking) for thirty minutes a day, but avoid heavy exercises or competitive sports.
6. Non-vigorous sexual intercourse is fine during pregnancy and, in fact, has a lower rate of pre-term labor compared to those who don't have sex.
7. Sex can be done in a prone position in the later months of pregnancy but should be gentle and non-coercive.
8. Avoid lying on your back in bed for more than fifteen minutes; instead lie on your right or left side to avoid compression of the

major abdominal blood vessels such as the aorta and the vena cava.

9. Always use your seat belt when driving and place it in a three-phase position emphasizing the lower belt under your belly and the cross belt above the abdomen.

10. Do not expose yourself to extreme temperatures to avoid complications from hypothermia or hyperthermia such as frostbite, heat exhaustion, or heat stroke.

11. Avoid flying in airplanes or traveling at high altitude levels after thirty-six weeks of pregnancy.

12. Avoid fried foods with high fat content as they worsen nausea and vomiting in the first trimester.

13. Eat an adequate amount of fruits and vegetables to counter the physiological effect of pregnancy that causes constipation.

14. Heavy sleep is normal during pregnancy and pregnant women should be encouraged to get an added two hours sleep each night.

15. Two to three pillows can be used when sleeping to avoid the physiological complications of nausea common in pregnancy.

16. Encourage slower and deeper breathing due to a reduced vital capacity of pregnancy.

17. Avoid high altitude environments because there will be decreased partial oxygen pressures (hypoxemia) as the pregnancy advances.

18. Avoid snakes, spiders, and other toxic agents as the anti-venoms required in severe cases could, on inoculation, complicate your pregnancy.

19. Avoid more than twelve ounces of tuna per week (to reduce potential complications due to mercury).

20. Breast tenderness is expected in early stages of pregnancy and is relieved by warm compress.

21. Vaginal secretions are commonly mistaken for infection or leakage of fluids. They are, however, thick, don't smell as much as infectious secretions, not profuse in quantity, and don't need treatment.

22. Avoid any over-the-counter medications and use only those approved by your Obstetrician/Family physician.

23. Don't forget to get your flu vaccine, especially if you will be pregnant during the flu season (October – March every year).

24. Back pain is common during pregnancy and back girdles have no proven efficacy. The only recommended option is Acetaminophen (at less than 3 gm per oral per day).

25. Non-steroidal anti-inflammatory or aspirin should not be used as they could cause premature patent ductus arteriousus (PDA) closure.

26. Increase your calcium intake during pregnancy as its deficiency may lead to osteomalacia or rickets in the fetus.

27. Calorie intake should include 150 extra calories per day in the first trimester and 300 to 500 extra calories per day in the last two trimesters.

28. Patients should wear light-fitting clothes as tight-fitting clothes could be uncomfortable and heat absorbing in pregnancy.

29. Patients shouldn't stand up for more than four hours at a time (in order to avoid varicose veins) and orthostatic hypotension.

30. Excessive straining during defecation can lead to external hemorrhoids and can be avoided by adequate fluid and eating fruits and vegetables.

31. Start taking oral folic acid 400 micrograms two months before conception, if you're planning your pregnancy. Take 1 gm if you had a previous neural tube defect baby.

32. Avoid exposure to ultra-violet or radioactive rays.

33. Do not take aluminum products like Pepcid as they bind to fetal bone.

34. The use of anti-emetics (like Ondansetron and Metoclopramide) are permitted in patients who are unable to keep food or fluid down in hypermemesis gravidarum.

35. Drink at least eight glasses of fluid daily.

36. Herpetic whitlow or herpetic stomatitis can be treated with acyclovir solution without endangering the life of the fetus.

37. Pruritic Urticarial Papules and Plaques of Pregnancy (PUPPP) is a dermatological condition that occurs in pregnancy but is self-resolving and does not need any intervention.

38. Topical steroid creams are non teratogenic and can be used in urticaria, severe PUPPP or jaundice of pregnancy.
39. Douching is not recommended as it leads to increased bacterial overgrowth and bacterial vaginosis.
40. A breast lump during pregnancy requires breast sonograms, not mammograms. This is because mammograms carry radioactive rays while sonograms do not. Also, a sonogram is more sensitive during pregnancy due to breast swelling.
41. In event of abdominal pains, an MRI scan of the abdomen is recommended, as it has no radioactive waves.
42. A dental visit prevents or diagnoses peri-partum gingivitis and consequently reduces the incidence of pre-term labor. This is because gingivitis increases the incidence of pre-term labor in pregnancy.
43. Treatment of Chlamydia during pregnancy with oral Azithromycin (doxycycline is contraindicated due to teeth chelation) reduces infection of the fetus with *Chlamydia Trachomatis* that causes opthalmia neonatorum and atypical neonatal pneumonia.
44. A social worker should see the pregnant patient at least once to ensure the suitability of her socio-economic and family environment.
45. Dental pathologies in pregnancy are treatable under local anesthesia but contra-indicated if general anesthesia is required.
46. Back pain is worsened by descent of the baby's head and can be relieved by tenderly massaging the back.
47. Bleeding from the vagina is an emergency at any time during pregnancy as it may connote miscarriage or pre-term labor.
48. Bed rest or stopping work have not been proven to reduce pre-term labor.
49. Where more than three early pre-term labors have occurred, a cervical cerclage is recommended.
50. Engender maternal fetal bonding and contraception by encouraging maternal breastfeeding pre-delivery.
51. Talk to any older children about the new baby to avoid confusion and issues at home.

52. Postpartum blues are symptoms of regret and lack of enthusiasm seen in 10 percent of postpartum women and should be investigated.

53. Postpartum depression occurs in 1 percent of postpartum patients and should be monitored for in patients with significant family history of depression or history of poor grooming during or after pregnancy. It can be treated successfully with Selective Serotonin Receptor Inhibitors (SSRI).

54. Postpartum psychosis is rare (0.1 percent) and associated with infanticide (murder of infants). It can be diagnosed postpartum in patients with disoriented and manic-like symptoms. This requires urgent hospitalization.

55. Pregnant patients above thirty-five years should undergo chorionic villus sampling (CVS) via amniocentesis and serum Alpha Feto Protein (AFP) assays. This is because older patients have higher chances of fetal teratogenicty or complications and these two sampling methods provide the most accurate measurement of the baby's health.

56. Pregnant patients with a history of migraines should avoid chocolates, wine, bright sunlight, or stress. Ergotamines and topiramates are contraindicated in pregnancy and pregnant patients with migraine are advised to treat their condition symptomatically with acetaminophen.

57. Life-threatening emergencies that involve the life of the mother, such as motor vehicle accidents, pelvic fractures, and bleeding, puts the mother's life at a precedent over that of the fetus.

58. A mucus plug is a common consequence of the late stages of pregnancy. It can be differentiated from amniotic fluid leakage by doing the fern and nitrazine test and so should not be confused with term rupture of membranes or leakage of fluids.

59. Do not expose a woman with confirmed premature Rupture of membranes (PROM) to more vaginal exams than necessary or poor hygiene. This leads to chorioamnionitis.

60. A Premature Preterm ruptured membrane (PPROM) patient should be admitted for surveillance and prophylactic steroid

administered (for development of lung surfactant in fetus) within seventy-two hours if fetus is less than thirty-four weeks of age.

61. Always give prophylactic antibiotics to a woman with ruptured membranes and fever to avoid fetal chorioamnionitis.

62. Always treat with appropriate antibiotics (such as macrobid, penicillin, amoxicillin, Cephalexin) if a patient's urine is positive for infection. This helps avoid the chance of developing pylenonephritis and this reduces the risk of triggering pre-term labor.

63. Do not use Quinolone anibiotics intra-partum. It leads to cartilage damage in the fetus.

64. Do not keep pets like turtles or rodents during pregnancy as they may cause salmonellosis.

65. Do not touch cat litter. This could lead to congenital toxoplasmosis.

66. Treat gonorrhea in pregnant patients with penicillin G or cephalosporin to avoid *opthalmia neonatorum gonorrhea.*

67. If (above) patient is allergic to penicillin, treat with Azithromycin.

68. Do not administer doxycycline to pregnant patients as it discolors the teeth of the fetus, when it eventually develops, permanently.

69. Urinalysis should be assessed at every antenatal visit for infection.

70. Every pregnant patient should be assessed with nuchal translucency (NT) sonogram, serum HCG and pregnancy associated plasma protein A (PAPP-A) at eleven to thirteen weeks of gestation. This determines any abnormalities such as Down's, Edward's, Patau, or Turner's syndrome.

71. A quad screen comprising B-HCG, alpha fetoprotein (AFP), inhibin-A and unconjugated estriol should be done at sixteen to eighteen weeks of gestation. This helps determine any predisposition to Downs, Turners, Edwards, Patau's syndrome, gastroschisis or even the presence of twins.

72. An integrated screening of first Trimester and second trimester diagnostic studies results in an improved 94-96 percent sensitivity in detecting Down's syndrome.

73. Fetal positioning changes up until thirty-six weeks gestation and after that requires Leopold maneuvering or external cephalic version if not in cephalic presentation.

74. The above maneuvers should not be done if patient has placenta previa or twin gestation.

75. A repeat lab test for Chlamydia, gonorrhea or syphilis should be done at thirty-six weeks gestational age of pregnancy. If positive, treat with penicillin and/or Azithromycin.

76. Anal intercourse is not contra-indicated in pregnancy but can be discomforting for the patient. It should be discouraged therefore.

77. Prenatal vitamins should be started as soon as possible at one tablet a day.

78. All vitamins are safe in pregnancy except excess Vitamin A which can cause cardiac, CNS, and craniofacial defects. These side effects occur when Vitamin A is consumed in excess of 8,000 IU/day.

79. Group B streptococcus should be treated prophylactically in pregnancy if found in urine. It should also be treated prophylactically, if at thirty-five weeks gestation, a vaginal swab culture on a pregnant patient grows penicillin G.

80. If above patient cannot take penicillin, patient must be desensitized and penicillin administered.

81. There will be cases of pica (a desire to eat non nutritive substances like ice, starch, clay and dirt) in pregnancy. This responds positively to iron supplementation.

82. Amniocentesis to diagnose Down's syndrome is done at fifteen to twenty weeks of gestation. This depends on quad screen titers and has a 0.5-1 percent chance of fetal loss.

83. Chorionic villus sampling is done at ten to twelve weeks gestation and has a risk of fetal loss of 1-2 percent.

84. Yellow eyes in a pregnant female is considered an emergency as it may be cholestasis of preganancy. This condition causes a higher incidence of meconium-stained amniotic fluid at delivery (25 percent of all cases), spontaneous preterm delivery (12.1 percent) and stillbirth.

85. Cholecystitis in pregnancy is not a surgical emergency and can be treated conservatively as long as it is not emphysematous or gangrenous gallbladder.

86. An infection of Rubella and Varicella during pregnancy could be deleterious to fetal well being. Strict contact isolation should be implemented especially in a home where a pregnant woman is not immune to these infections and there is an index case of Chicken pox (varicella) or Rubella in the premises.

87. Patients with a high risk for hepatitis C (such as IVDA or multiple blood transfusions) should be tested for hepatitis antibodies and, if positive, be vaccinated against Hepatitis A/B, counseled on the 3-10 percent chance of transmitting infection to fetus, and on the need to avoid such high risk behavior.

88. A woman who is a vegetarian or has low hemoglobin baseline should be evaluated for iron stores and if low started on ferrous gluconate supplements.

89. Multiple swellings on the front of bilateral legs (erythema nodosum) are not uncommon in pregnancy and require only topical steroids if recalcitrant.

90. Systemic lupus erythematotus (SLE) can cause congenital heart block if uncontrolled and current guidelines recommend stabilization of the lupus female, clinically, before attempting conception.

91. Cytomegalovirus (CMV) infection can be transmitted materno-fetally via the placenta and mothers with symptoms suggestive of CMV (especially immuno-compromised patients) should be treated with CMV immunoglobulins.

92. Melasma (shades on the cheeks) are worsened by sunlight and is a physiological response to pregnancy.

93. Isotretinoin (Accutane) should not be used in pregnancy.

94. Do not take whirlpool or public tub baths as it increases susceptibility to vaginal infections.

95. Alcohol is contra-indicated in pregnancy as it can cause fetal alcohol syndrome.

96. The earlier you get a sonographic image of pregnancy, the more accurate the fetal age.

97. Blood pressure should be at its lowest during your second trimester—about 90/60 mm hg—and does not require any intervention.

98. White blood cell counts are elevated in pregnancy and should not cause alarm (especially during labor) unless it is above 15,000/mm.

99. Pregnant women at risk for CMV infection (such as day care workers, mothers with a toddler in day care or health care workers) should wash their hands extensively and use gloves when changing diapers. This is especially true if they are CMV seronegative.

100. No form of physical or emotional abuse should be tolerated. Any abuse must be reported immediately to the appropriate authorities.

Delivery of a newborn is 1 percent human perspiration and 99 percent heavenly inspiration.

CHAPTER 8

Blunders in Birthing!

By thee have I been holden up from the womb: thou art
He that took me out of my mother's bowels.
—Psalm 71:6

If you want a successful delivery, you must prepare for it. God is the architect, but He uses human agents. In delivery, the first thing to prepare for is labor. Labor is the onset of regular, rhythmic contractions that lead to dilatation and effacement of the cervix. It is described by knowledgeable physicians as "99 percent inspiration and 1 percent perspiration" because for the most part God is the one at work!

The current maternal mortality rate ranges from eleven per one hundred thousand in the United States to sixteen hundred per one hundred thousand in Afghanistan. This difference occurs because there is poverty, lack of access and insufficient ante-partum care amongst pregnant women in the third world. What takes the lives of most mothers at the birthing process can be prevented if some of the points enumerated below are implemented.

Common Blunders in Birthing!

1. Waiting beyond forty-two weeks gestational age to deliver a newborn.

2. Delivering a macrosomic baby (greater than 3.5 kg) without considering use of Assisted Delivery Techniques (ADTs). ADTs include forceps or vacuum delivery. Their absence may lead to high-risk complications such as Erb's paly, clavicular fractures or maternal third-degree perineal tears.

3. A Rhesus negative mother who does not receive a Rhogam isoimmunization injection at twenty weeks is a blunder. Also, she should receive another Rhogam injection immediately after birth as this prevents hemolytic disease of the newborn from the sensitized maternal rhesus antibodies.

4. Not receiving an oxytocin analogue (like pitocin) after the delivery of the right shoulder) as a precaution against postpartum hemorrhage (PPH) is another blunder.

5. Incomplete delivery of the placenta is a common blunder. This leads to PPH if retained for more than one hour.

6. Eating foods twelve hours before delivery can lead to fatal complications like aspiration pneumonitis.

7. Walking long distances at term is a common blunder. Many believe it quickens onset of labor. On the contrary, it strains you and does nothing to quicken the onset of labor.

8. Excessive weight gain during pregnancy is a blunder. Some think they are eating for two and overindulge. Obesity in pregnancy (anything above a weight gain of forty pounds during the pregnancy period) causes more complications at delivery and is harmful to the baby.

9. Not using assisted delivery techniques (like forceps and vacuums) when signs of fetal distress, like meconium or variable/late decelerations appear, is a common blunder. Those signs of fetal distress demand immediate intervention.

10. Ignoring symptoms like headaches, photophobia (seeing stars), and abdominal pain in a late trimester pregnant woman is a blunder. They may be telltale signs, along with elevated blood pressure, of Pre-eclampsia.

11. Ignoring symptoms like vaginal bleeding associated with abdominal pain is a blunder. These may be indicative of a condition like *abruption placentae*.

12. Utilizing a delivery position such as the ventral lithotomy position (laying on your stomach) is a common blunder. Current research points to the upright position during the second stage of labor as the most comfortable for the patient.

13. More than twenty-four hours of labor in any pregnancy is prolonged but, unfortunately, a common blunder. Such prolonged labor may require assisted delivery techniques or augmentation of labor.

14. Delivering a fetus while immersed in water is a common blunder. It has no credible studies to show it is safer or better than normal delivery.

15. Delivering a mal-positioned fetus (such as one in the occipitoposterior position) vaginally. This is the most common cause of arrest on descent in labor and should be resolved by ADTs intervention or cesarean section. Occipito-anterior positions in the fetus, on the other hand, are the most favorable position for a term vaginal delivery.

16. Delaying fetal delivery beyond one hour of full dilation of the cervix may jeopardize the health of the fetus.

17. Delaying a placenta delivery beyond half an hour of fetal delivery may lead to PPH.

18. Having a blood loss above 500 ml (after vaginal delivery) or one liter (after cesarean section) within twenty-four hours without the required hemoglobin monitoring is a blunder. The transfusion of blood products could save the pregnant patient developing severe anemia and if unabated hemolytic shock or death.

19. Ignoring a drop in hemoglobin of more than three mg/dl post-delivery is an unacceptable blunder. This drop is inimical to the life of the mother and if confirmed requires blood transfusion.

20. Ignoring postpartum hemorrhage (PPH) instead of identifying the source and administring methylergonovine (a vasoconstrictor) is a common blunder in PPH. In emergencies, an abdominal hysterectomy may even be required.

21. Not speaking about back pain preterm is a common blunder. This leads to an unprepared patient at term; it makes her

uninformed about what analgesic methods are available and what to request.

22. Unawareness of the patient that the use of epidural analgesia can double the time of delivery is a common blunder. It increases the time for stage two (delivery of fetus period) due to poor contractility.

23. Use of intramuscular analgesics six hours before delivery, though common, is a blunder that may cause over sedation of the fetus on delivery.

24. Prolonged straining during labor can lead to hemorrhoids. Experts may recommend suppositories prior to delivery if bowel movements are already difficult.

25. Confusing Braxton Hicks contractions (which last up to ten to thirty minutes and are not sharp or rhythmic) with labor pains (which are regular, contractile, and last ten to fifteen minutes) is a common blunder.

26. In event of a macrosomic fetus, not utilizing the MacRoberts maneuver is a common blunder during delivery. This maneuver involves elevating the thighs up to the abdomen and applying supra-abdominal pressure. The non-use of this maneuver leads to complications such as a cyanotic baby, distressed or fractured collar bones secondary to shoulder dystocia and injured viscera.

27. Confusing a mucus plug with leakage of amniotic fluid is a common blunder at term. This makes for a wrong determination of labor. The confirmatory test for amniotic fluid leakage includes a fern or the nitrazine test slide.

28. Restricting the presence of the patient's partner in the delivery room is a common blunder. This can hamper good outcomes as holding a pregnant wife's hands or rubbing her back have been found beneficial in the delivery process.

29. Taking water up to six hours before cesarean delivery can endanger the mother's life. This common blunder can cause death by aspiration pneumonitis.

30. Not placing a nasogastric tube in a woman who ate less than six hours ago, in order to empty the abdomen and avoid aspiration

pneumonitis before undergoing an emergency cesarean section is another common blunder.

31. Not giving peri-partum antibiotics before cesarean section delivery is a common blunder in third world countries. This leads to increased risk of endometritis and maternal infection.

32. Not applying oxygen via nasal cannula to the mother during delivery is another common blunder. This impairs oxygen delivery to the fetus and leads to a baby born with respiratory distress.

33. Not administering intravenous fluids (preferably isotonic) during delivery is another common blunder. The adequate hydration of the mother (and consequently the fetus) helps ensure electrolyte and biomedical balance at birth.

34. Not routinely assessing amniotic fluid levels (in combination with non stress tests and fetal monitoring) in a term pregnancy lead to poor outcomes as they measure fetal stability *in utero*.

35. Not calculating the bishop score (which includes effacement, dilatation of cervix, station, consistency and position) prior to augmentation of labor is a common blunder. This ensures the suitability of labor per vagina.

36. Not discussing post-partum issues, like contraception, before delivery is a blunder. This early introduction could afford the patient an opportunity of including an elective tubal ligation postpartum or during a cesarean section.

37. A major blunder that hampers breastfeeding postpartum is the lack of information given to expectant mothers on what feeding technique the mother will implement on delivery. A lack of awareness on the advantages of breastfeeding has seen an increase in formula fed neonates and infants in the last decade.

38. Not encouraging rooming in, of mother and baby, on delivery is another common blunder of birthing. This encourages bottle-feeding with formula at the expense of breastfeeding.

39. Not having a physician with expertise in c-section within thirty minutes' reach of labor room when a Vaginal Birth After Cesarean section (VBAC) patient undergoes vaginal delivery is a major blunder and contravenes current American College of Obstetrics and Gynecology (ACOG) guidelines.

40. Attempting a vaginal delivery in multiple gestation, mal-presentation, or mal-positioned fetus can lead to complications or fatalities in pregnancy deliveries. They may lead to arrest of labor, arrest of descent or fetal distress.

41. Pelvimetry (that is calculated pelvic dimensions) is not sufficient to determine the suitability of a cervix. Only trial of labor with a prior pregnancy is sufficient.

42. Ignoring the loss of uterine contour or palpable fetal parts could be a fatal blunder. This sign is the most common presenting sign of a ruptured uterus.

43. Insufficient monitoring of the fetus with a fetal monitor during VBAC is another common blunder.

44. Over dependence on fetal monitors may also be another common blunder. This is because it has been shown to lead to an increased number of cesarean sections.

45. A non-examination for all parts of the placenta is a common blunder that could lead to a retained placenta. This also heightens the risk for PPH.

46. In a pre-eclamptic patient, not evaluating the placenta for necrosis or ischemia, is a blunder that fails to pin point etiology and pathology of the condition.

47. In a patient who presents with failure to lactate post-partum, Sheehan syndrome secondary to PPH must be investigated. A lack of investigation is a blunder of birthing.

48. A fetus that develops sub-conjuctival hemorrhage postpartum could be misdiagnosed as fetal abuse or attempted infanticide victim. This commonly occurs from labor and re-assurance is all that is needed.

49. Not continuing folic acid, ferrous gluconate, and vitamins for two months after maternal delivery is a common blunder. This impairs the replenishment of those stores that were lost during delivery.

50. Traveling within one to two days of delivery is a common and increasingly fatal blunder. This increases the chance of developing a Deep Venous Thromboses (DVT) or pulmonary embolus.

51. Not emptying the bladder with a urinary catheter during labor is a common blunder. It obstructs delivery or parturition and so delays the second part of labor.

52. Birthing in pools. Though not contra-indicated, it shows no benefit compared to regular deliveries.

53. Keeping contact lenses in while delivering a baby could be a blunder. The contact lens can grow uncomfortable during pregnancy as corneal thickness increases progressively. They are better removed during pregnancy.

54. Precipitous labor (delivering without head control) leads to increased intracranial hemorrhage and clavicle fractures and is, unfortunately, a common blunder.

55. Not educating the patient on labor contractions and when to push during labor is a common blunder. These wrongful contractions of the mid pelvis leads to cephalopelvic disproportion and fetal demise.

56. Ignoring an Umbilical cord prolapse can cause impaired cephalad circulation of blood and fetal mortality. Ignoring the presentation of an umbilical cord per-vagina is foolhardy and requires emergent cesarean section.

57. Doing an episiotomy medially is a common but needless blunder. This incision can cause increased chance of lacerating the external anal sphincter. The medio-lateral episiotomy is the recommended incision when an episiotomy must be done.

58. A patient with Group B Streptococcus (GBS) positive culture (after thirty-five weeks gestation) or with unknown GBS status, requires intravenous Penicillin antibiotics prior to delivery. The lack of treatment causes GBS sepsis or meningitis in the baby.

59. Not evaluating for sexually transmitted infections such as HIV, syphilis, Chlamydia, or Gonorrhea in the third trimester leads to fetal complications like Chlamydia neonatorum, neonatal syphilis, or atypical pneumonia in newborns.

60. A patient with a past history of delivering a fetus with GBS sepsis, pneumonia, or meningitis in a prior pregnancy must automatically receive the intravenous prophylactic antibiotic at term in the current pregnancy. Not doing so is a common blunder of birthing.

Increase is the hallmark insignia of God's kingdom.

CHAPTER 9

Starting a House

[A]nd God dealt well with the midwives because they
feared God and He made them houses.
—Exodus 1:21

More newborns die between birth and the first six weeks of life
that at any other time of their life.

During the neonatal period (first four weeks after birth), death is
most common among children that were born preterm, have low birth
weights, and have complications from pregnancy including placenta,
umbilicus, and membrane abnormalities.

The most common causes of neonatal death are chromosomal
abnormalities, preterm births, and Sudden Infant Distress Syndrome
(SIDS). Together they accounted for more than ten thousand neonatal
deaths in the United States in 2008.

The Puerperium Principles

Some essential things to starting a house with a newborn
include:

1. Delaying postpartum tubal ligation by eight to twelve hours, for
    cardiovascular stabilization, if delivered by spontaneous vaginal
    delivery.

2. Exclusive breastfeeding is recommended as it promotes mother-baby bonding, increases immunoglobulin deposition and neonatal immunity, and ensures inhibition of ovulation for the first ten weeks postpartum.

3. Postpartum deep venous thromboses (DVT) are highest two weeks after delivery, due to impaired mobility and increased vessel trauma. It is therefore not recommended to travel by air during this period. Increased ambulation at this point is a plus to health.

4. Starting breastfeeding postpartum encourages colostrum (the first secretion postpartum from the breast milk) feeding of the neonate. This secretion contains more minerals and immunoglobulins than breast milk.

5. The new mother should take at least 1,500 mg of calcium daily. This augments her breastfeeding and enables greater lactation to take place.

6. Breastfeed the newborn as it reduces breast engorgement in postpartum mothers. This reduces the risk of developing mastitis.

7. Every mother should receive adequate information on breastfeeding techniques, as this ensures that both the foremilk, which is rich in proteins, carbohydrates, and water and the hind milk, which is rich in fat, are both administered.

8. Administer vitamin K to newborn babies. It is absent in breast and formula milk and in its deficient state, could lead to easy bleeding in the newborn.

9. Avoid sex for at least six weeks after delivery to ensure adequate uterine involution and perineal healing.

10. Genital warts are not a contra-indication to vaginal delivery and can be treated post-partum. A rare complication to be aware of is laryngeal papillomatosis in the delivered fetus due to inadvertent ingestion of papillomas during delivery.

11. Post-partum rooming in with a baby, for at least two days, is highly encouraged as it encourages breastfeeding and bonding.

12. Positive hepatitis B patients should have their baby vaccinated with a hepatitis B vaccine within twenty-four hours of birth, and

with a hepatitis B immunoglobulin if the mother had elevated viral loads.

13. Live vaccines like mumps, rubella, measles and varicella can be administered to the mother after delivery, as long as there are no contraindications to receiving them.

14. Always maintain postpartum hematocrit (HCT) above 30 percent.

15. The new mother should avoid long hours of standing, especially if she has PPH as she may develop orthostatic hypotension secondary to anemia and hypovolemia.

16. Always administer antibiotic ointment to the fetus eyes on delivery. This will prevent *opthalmia neonatorum*.

When you stand for what you believe in,
it won't be long before you quit standing.

CHAPTER 10

When All Else Fails

Wherefore take unto you the whole armor of God, that
ye may be able to withstand in the evil day, and having
done all, to stand.
—Ephesians 6:13

When all else fails, the blood of Jesus never fails! Revelation 12:11 says, "we overcome the devil by the blood of the lamb and by the word of our testimony (for) we loved not our lives unto death." The blood of Jesus is the guarantee that no sin can remain in our lives and assures us that, in spite of past misdemeanors or experiences, He has "separated our sins from us as far as the east is from the west" (Psalm 103:12).

In the story of Samson (see Judges 16) we are told that "Samson said unto the lad that held him by the hand, suffer me that I may feel the pillars whereupon the house stands" (Judges 16:26) because he was blind! If he had not been blind, he would not have been placed by the two most powerful pillars in the house of the Philistine god Dagon leading "the dead which he slew at his death (to be) more than they which he slew in his life" (Judges 16:30). He killed more people in his death than while alive because he decided to turn his disability into a power portal to hurt Satan.

You can hurt the Devil by your testimony and your lifestyle even in the middle of your adversity. Romans 8:28 says, "all things work together for good to them that love God, to them who are the called according to his purpose."

Six F's while waiting for your pregnancy!

1) Faith

Romans 4:19-20 says that Abraham "being not weak in faith considered not his own body now dead, when he was about an hundred years old, neither yet the deadness of Sarah's womb (but) staggered not at the promise of God through unbelief but was strong in faith giving glory to God." He transformed his weak body into a reservoir of life by never quitting his faith in God! He had several opportunities to change his opinion but did not take them because he believed in God. When you stand for what you believe in, it won't be long before you quit standing. The power to Abraham's faith was God who "calls those things which be not as though they were" (Romans 4:16).

2) Fearlessness

In Exodus 1:20, God made the Hebrew midwives' houses because they feared God. They chose to obey God rather than Pharoah who wanted them to kill the Hebrew children. Likewise, He will bless us if we walk in the fear of the Lord and remain fearless.

In the fear of the Lord is strong confidence and his children shall have a place of refuge. The fear of the Lord is a "fountain of life to depart from the snares of death" (Proverbs 14:26-27). Nothing can stop a woman who fears nothing and nobody but God. Proverbs 19:23 says that "the fear of the Lord tends to life and he that it shall abide satisfied (and) shall not be visited with evil."

3) Faithfulness

Keep doing what you are doing and keep speaking what you are saying and God will vindicate you. Hebrews 10:35-36 says, "cast not away therefore your confidence, which hath great recompense of reward for ye have need of patience that after ye have done the will of God ye might receive the promise."

Too many people quit too soon, and often it is just when their miracle is about to manifest. It is at the point of greatest resistance that the breakthrough bursts forth, and at the darkest time of the night that daylight shines forth.

It is important to continue in well doing if you are to experience true freedom. Jesus said in John 8:31-32 that "if we continue in His word then are we His disciples indeed and we shall know the truth and the truth shall make us free." It is not enough to intermittently live healthy, or do the right things to become pregnant, but you should always live according to His Word. If you stay faithful, He will make you His demonstration project to the world of what God can do!

4) Fullness of Joy

Every pregnancy has a delivery date and every problem has an expiration date! The Bible tells us in Psalm 126:6 that "he that goes forth weeping, bearing precious seed, shall doubtless come again with rejoicing, bringing his sheaves with him." Sorrow is your enemy: it cripples your faith and prayer life.

Hannah was bitter and barren. She was enmeshed in "bitterness of soul and prayed unto the Lord and wept sore" (1 Samuel 1:10). Her barrenness persisted until one day "her countenance was no more sad and (she) worshipped the Lord and Elkanah knew Hannah his wife and the Lord remembered her" (1 Samuel 1:18-19).

Joy is our entry point into God's presence (Psalm 100:4). Without it, we can't soar like God wants. Isaiah 54:1 says, "Sing, O barren, thou that didst not bear; break forth into singing, and cry aloud, thou that didst not travail with child: for more are the children of the desolate than the children of the married wife."

5) Fulfilling God's Purpose

Your becoming pregnant is not to massage your ego or to fill a void only God can fill; it is not about making your husband love you more, but fulfilling God's ultimate purpose for humanity on creation (Genesis 1:26).

Leah thought that having more children would cement her relationship with Jacob (her husband) but died heartbroken after giving him six children, including his only daughter. In Genesis 29:34, she said, "now will my husband be joined unto me because I have born him three sons." This wasn't the case, as Jacob still loved Rachel more.

Children can never satisfy—only Jesus satisfies! Children are "a heritage of the Lord, His reward (and) arrows in the hand of a mighty man" (Psalm 127:3-4). They will not make you justified or place you in the plan of God for your life, but give continuity and multiplication, according to Genesis 1:28, to the nations.

6) Fellowship

One thing that brings people together is problems! The reason for this camaraderie is that you can comfort people going through similar conditions. Apostle Paul said in 2 Corinthians 1:4 that "who comforts us in all our tribulation, that we may be able to comfort them which are in any trouble, by the comfort wherewith we ourselves are comforted of God."

Barrenness is not just about you but for all those going through the heartache of barrenness that God is concerned about. He wants you to, after encountering a woman with a long period of childlessness or recurrent miscarriage, have the ability to respond to her heart pangs adequately.

The Bible teaches us in Galatians 6:7 that "whatsoever a man sows that shall he also reap." If you want children, sow into children and reap yours! In the beginning of the salvation story, God wanted a family and gave His son—Jesus—and so if you want children, invest in children spiritually, financially, emotionally, and physically.

Investing in children entails supporting children's causes, hosting families, mentoring them, and building orphanages for those in need. This will act as a seed for your future harvest as you trust God for your own children. Remember Proverbs 11:24 says that "he that waters shall be watered also himself." Expect your children today!